⊷ 1897 ⊶
CHARTS FOR NEEDLEPOINT COUNTED CROSS STI

OUVERAGES DE DAMES
ALPHABETS FROM 19TH CENTURY PARIS

This little French book is a compilation of patterns published previously as the more common smaller fold-out booklets– it's one of the few hardcover books of this kind that I've ever found.

Line-drawn alphabets were transferred onto fabric for surface embroidery, very often using padded satin stitches for whitework monograms on items such as household linens. Charted motifs were originally intended for netting (a lace technique) or filet crochet (which mimics netted lace) but are equally suitable for needlepoint and counted cross stitch.

A very interesting aspect of may of these charts is that the letters and motifs offer two ways of working them: "silhouette" style, worked with a single color, or "shaded" by using a second color to create depth and shadow. A reproducible sheet of graph paper is included to aid you in creating your own designs with these charts.

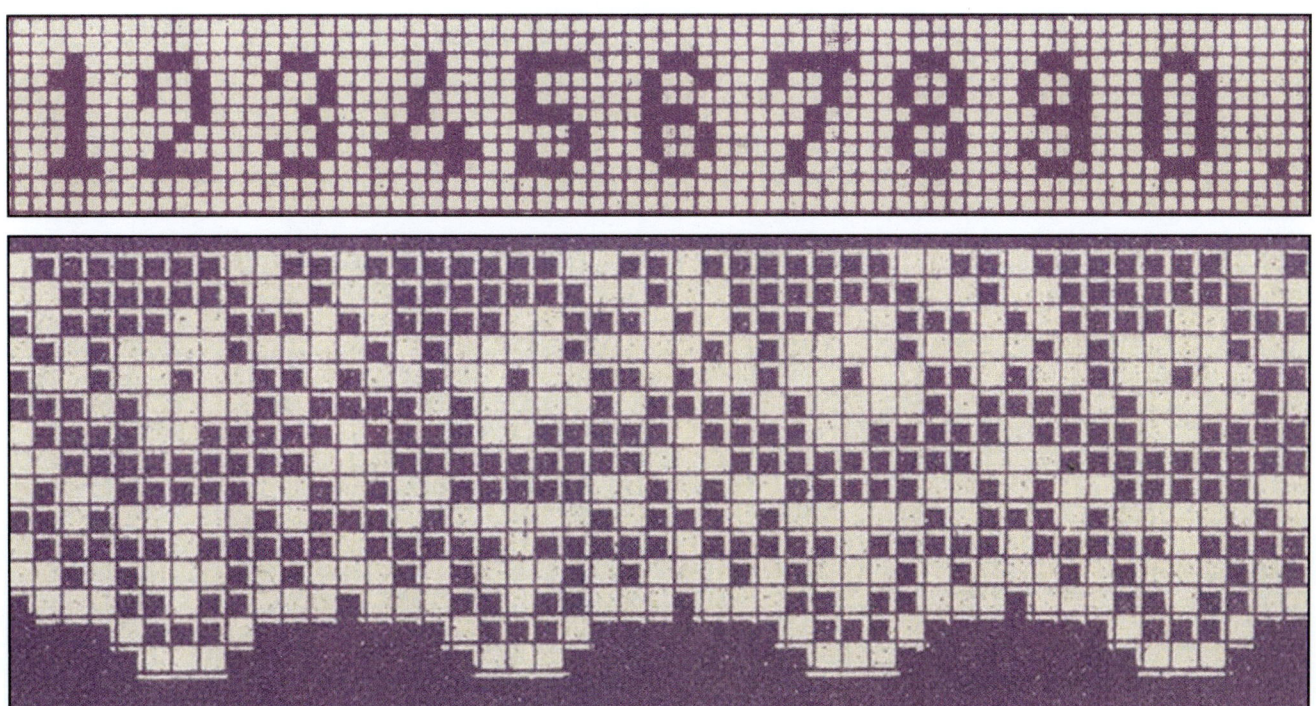

ALPHABETS FROM 19TH CENTURY PARIS©

ALPHABETS from 19th CENTURY PARIS©
© 2020 by Susan Johnson for SJ Designs

All rights reserved. No part of these instructions, charts or images may be reproduced in any form, including but not limited to photocopying and scanning, without written permission. Visit Susan at www.sj-designs.com.

ALPHABETS from 19th CENTURY PARIS

ALPHABETS from 19th CENTURY PARIS

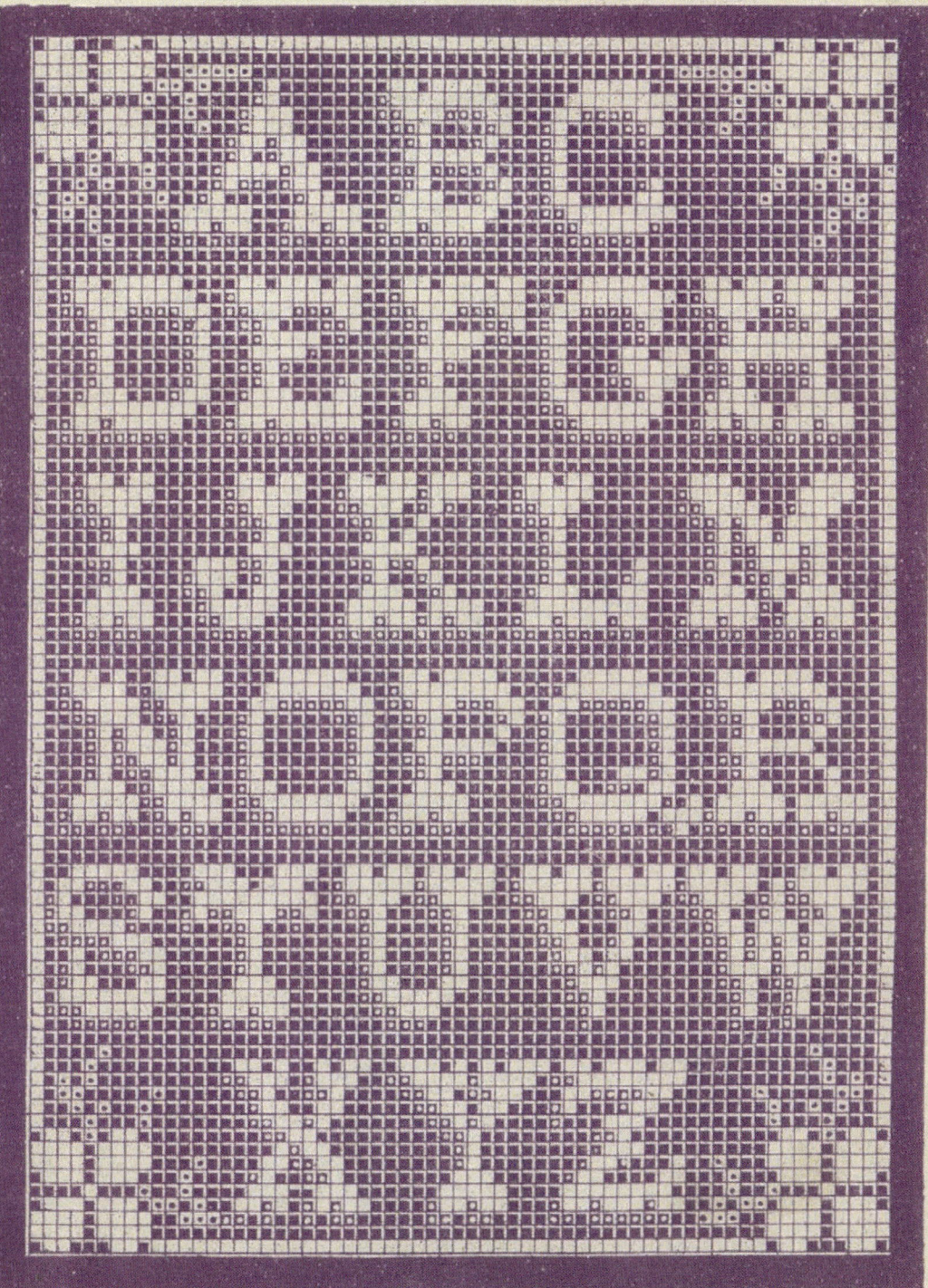

ALPHABETS FROM 19th CENTURY PARIS©

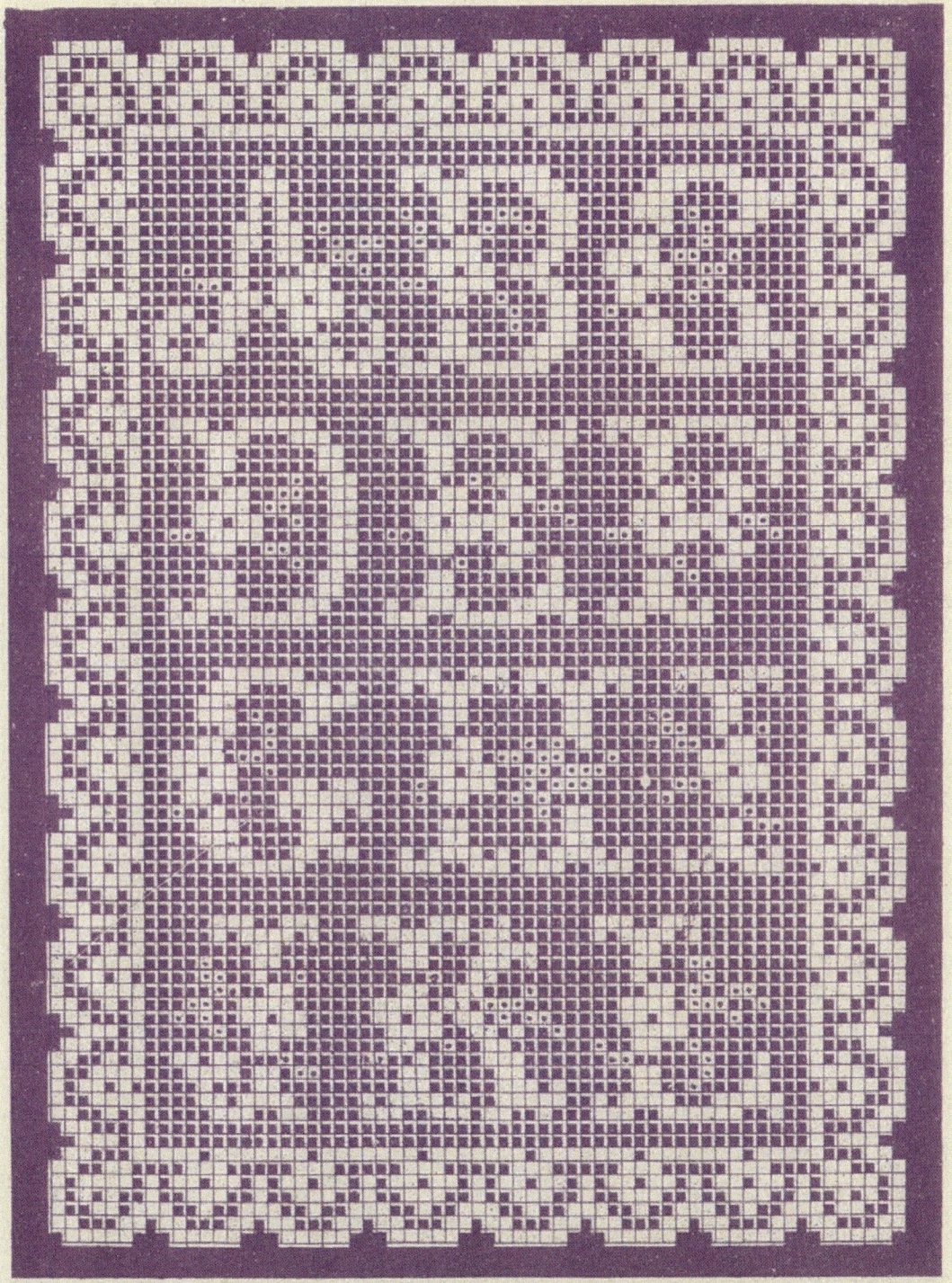

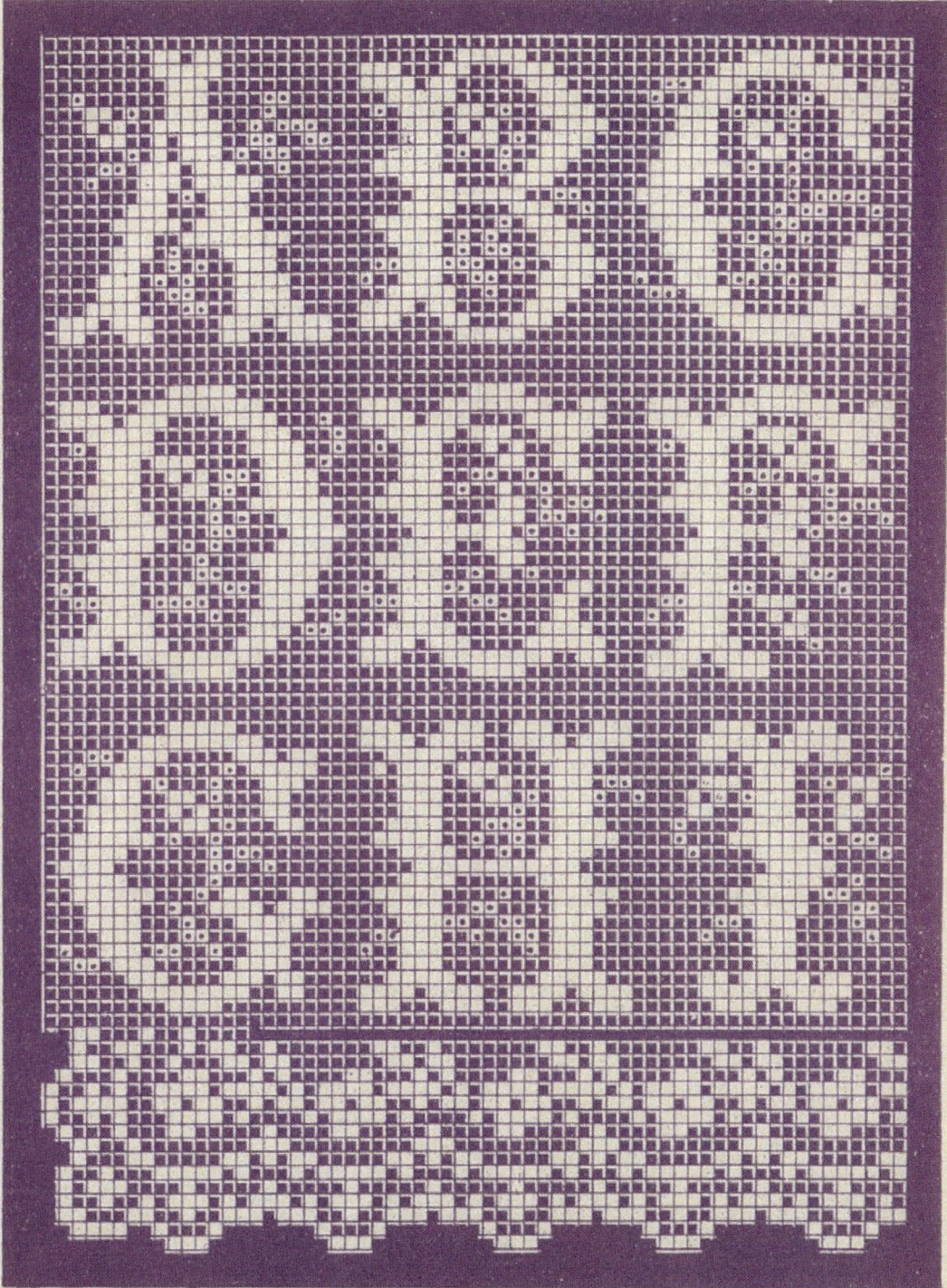

ALPHABETS from 19th CENTURY PARIS

Propriété exclusive de la Manufacture Parisienne des COTONS L. V.

ALPHABETS from 19th CENTURY PARIS

Propriété exclusive de la Manufacture Parisienne des COTONS L. V.

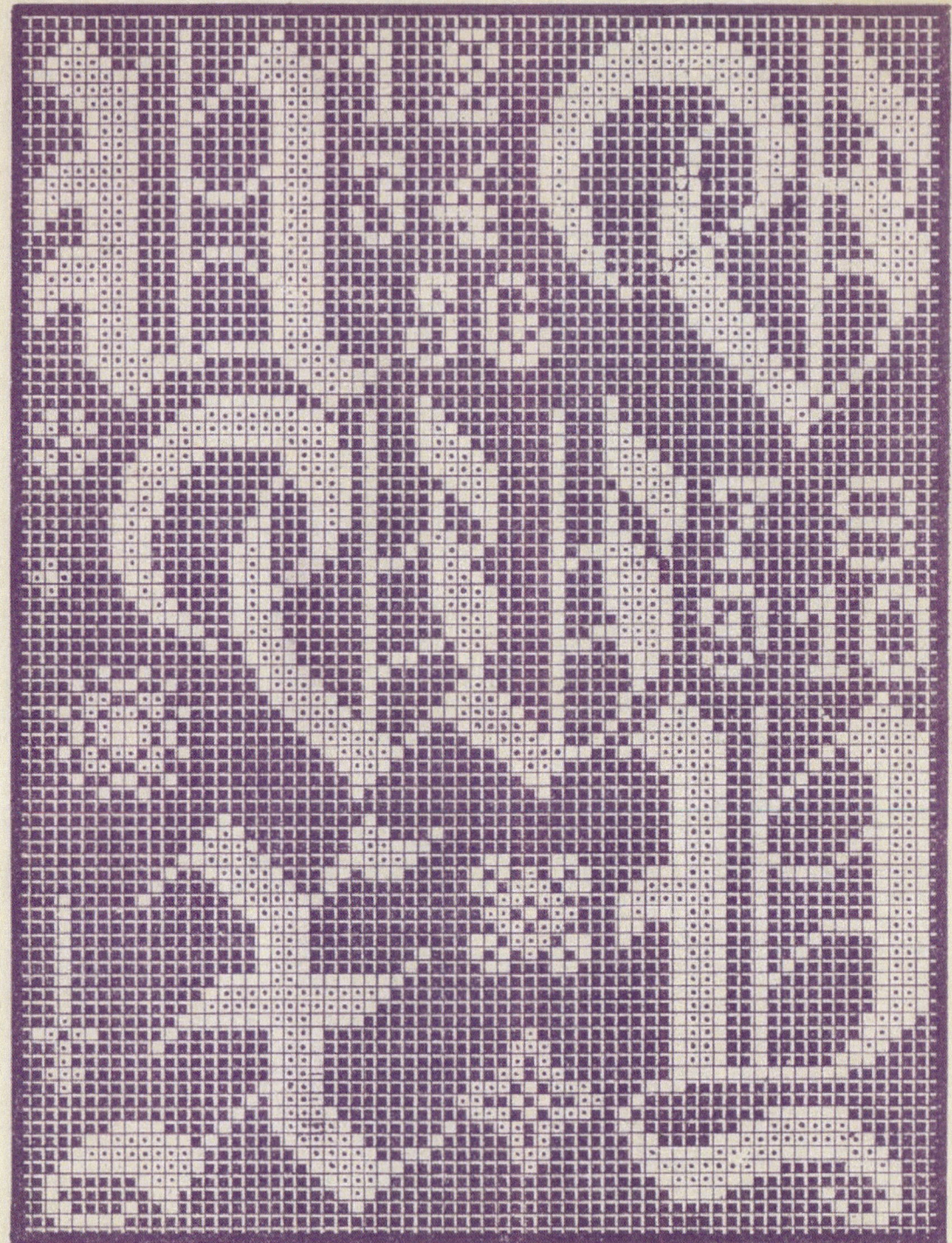

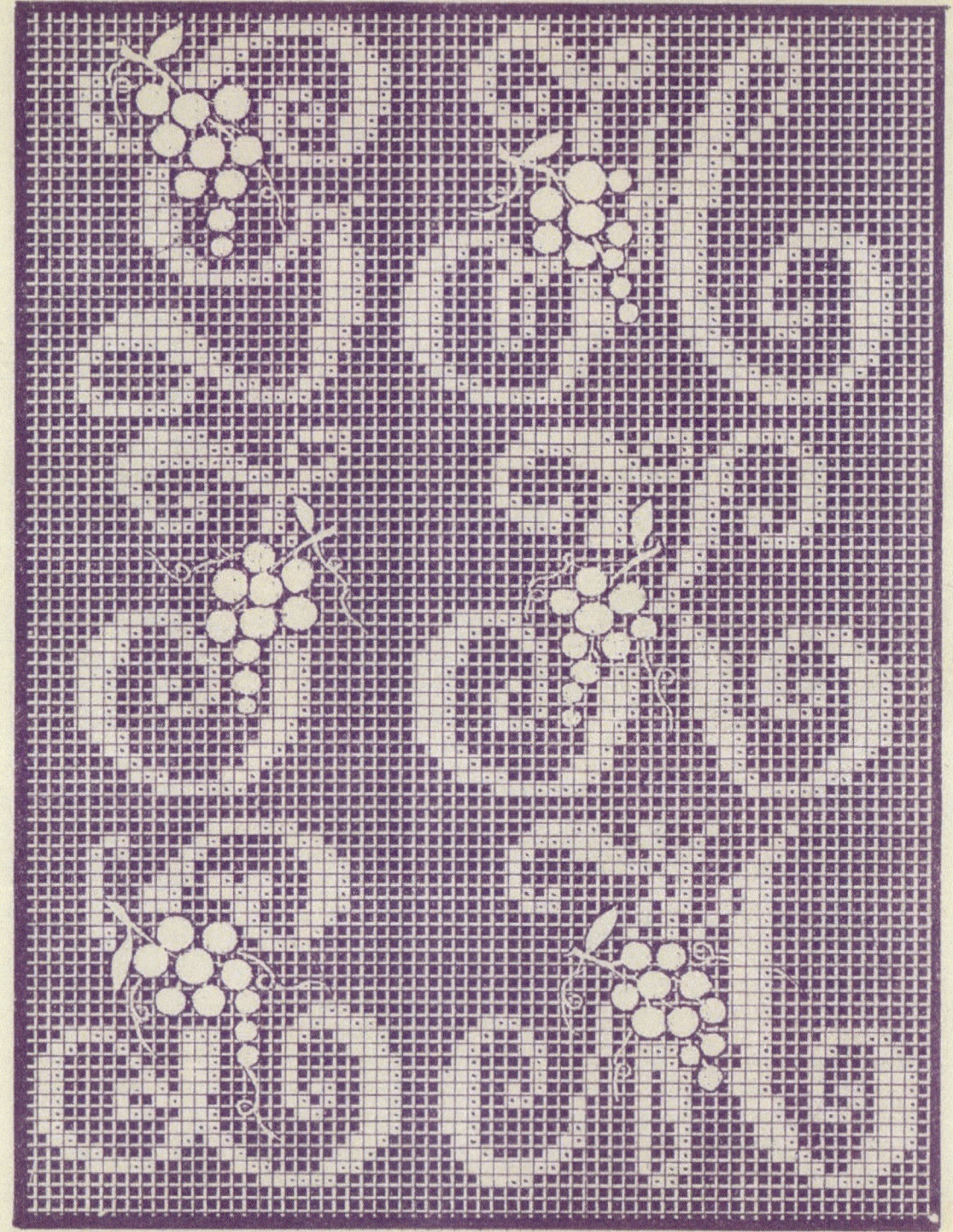

19th CENTURY CHARTED ALPHABETS from EUROPE©

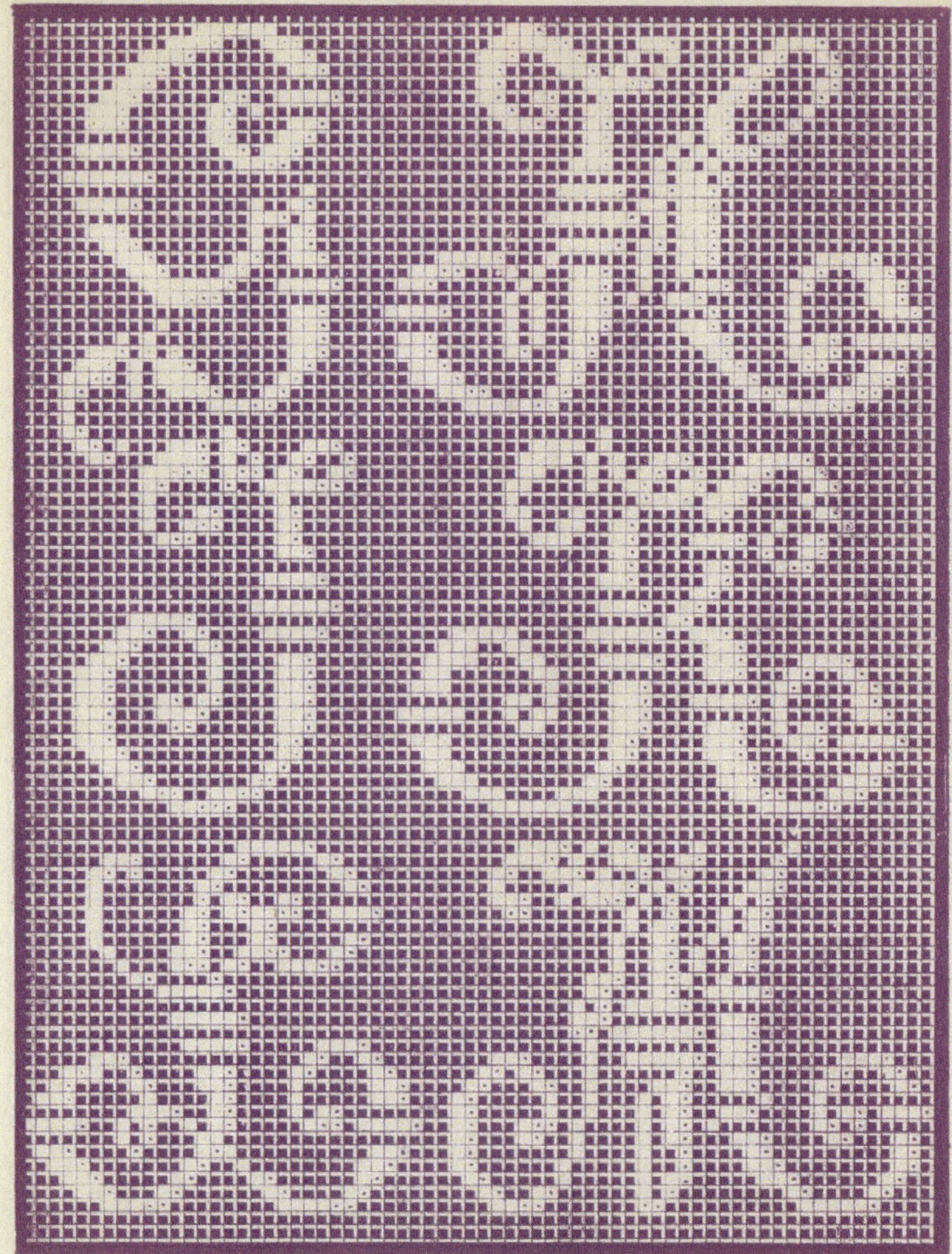

19th CENTURY CHARTED ALPHABETS from EUROPE

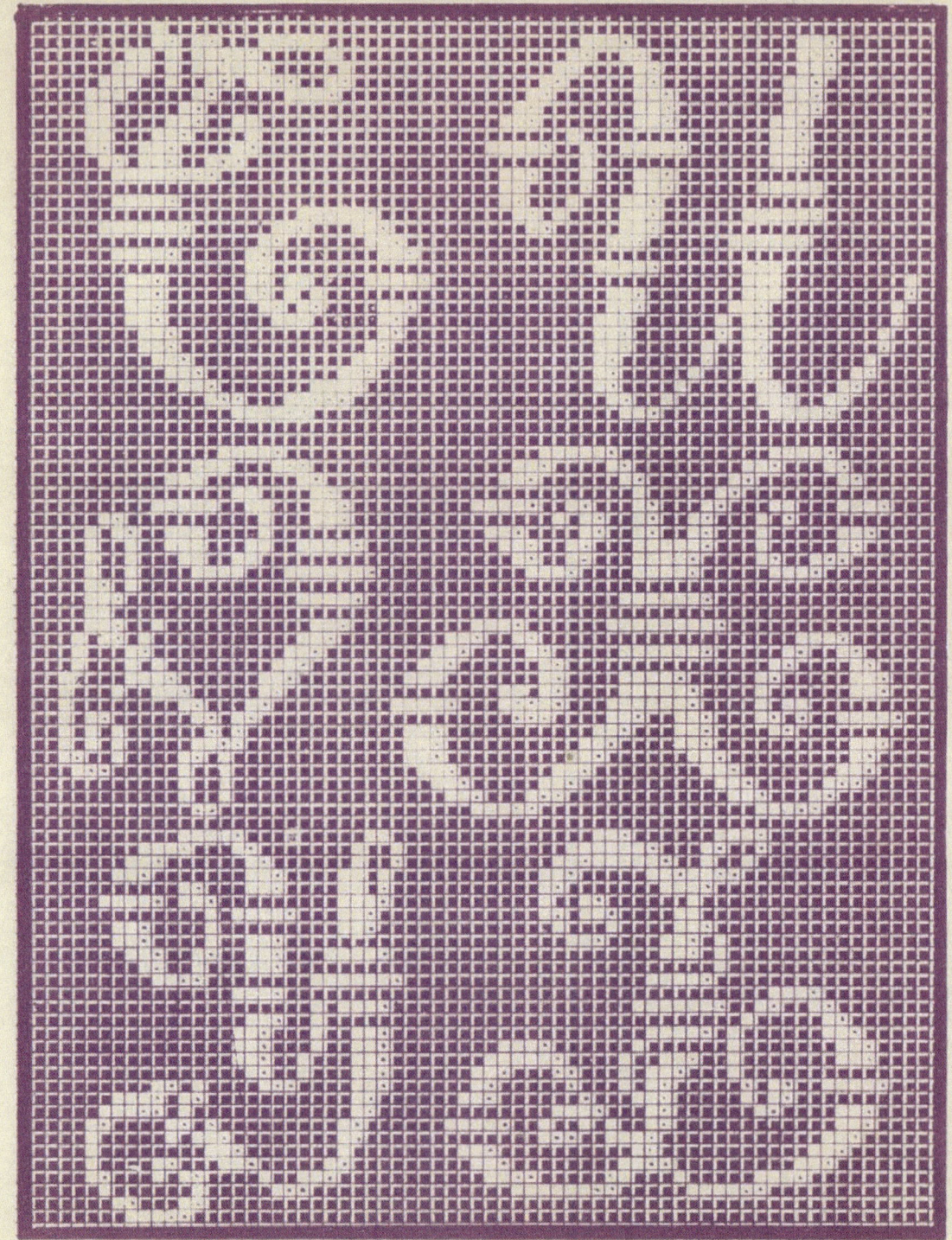

19th Century Charted Alphabets from Europe

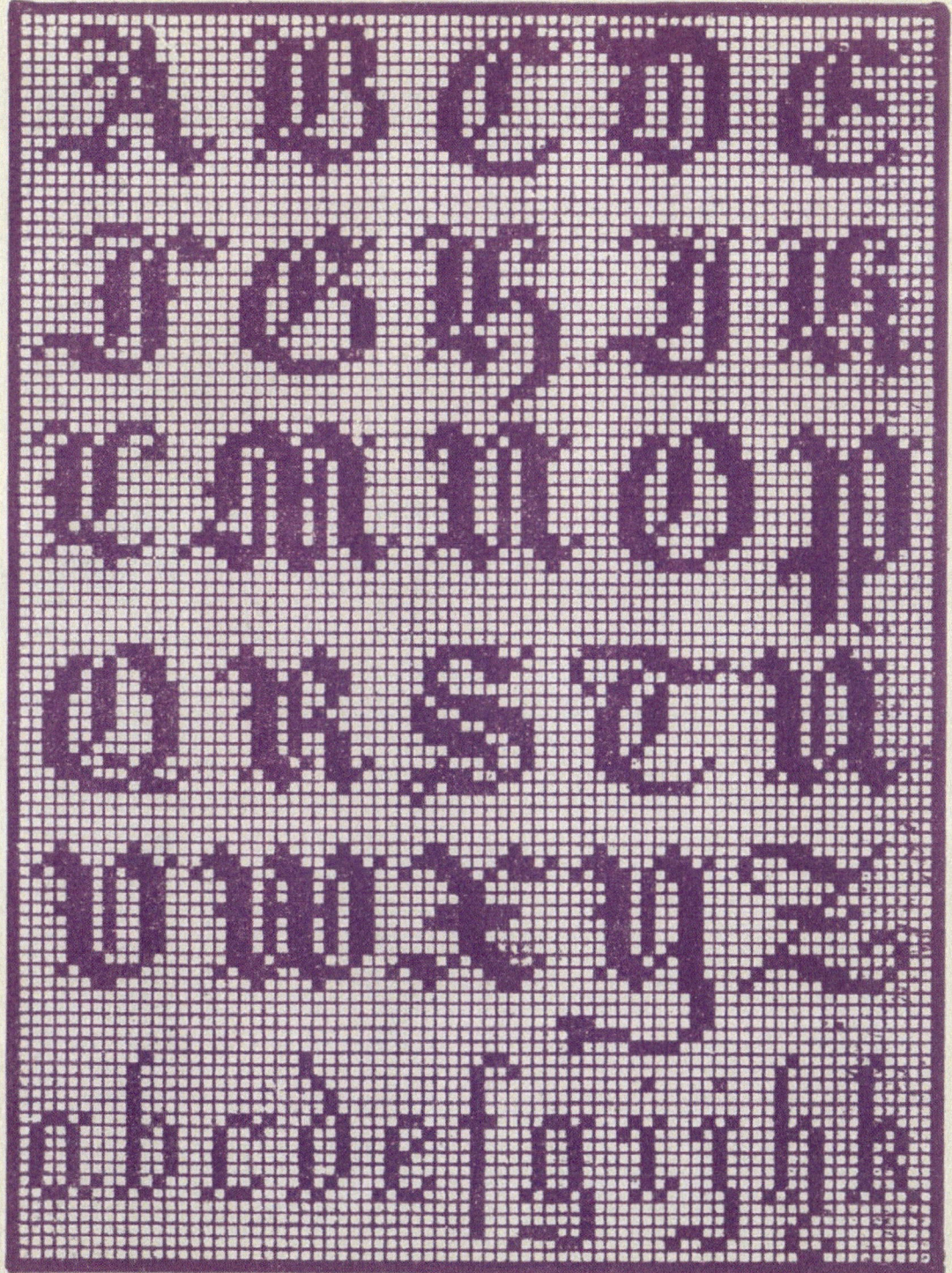

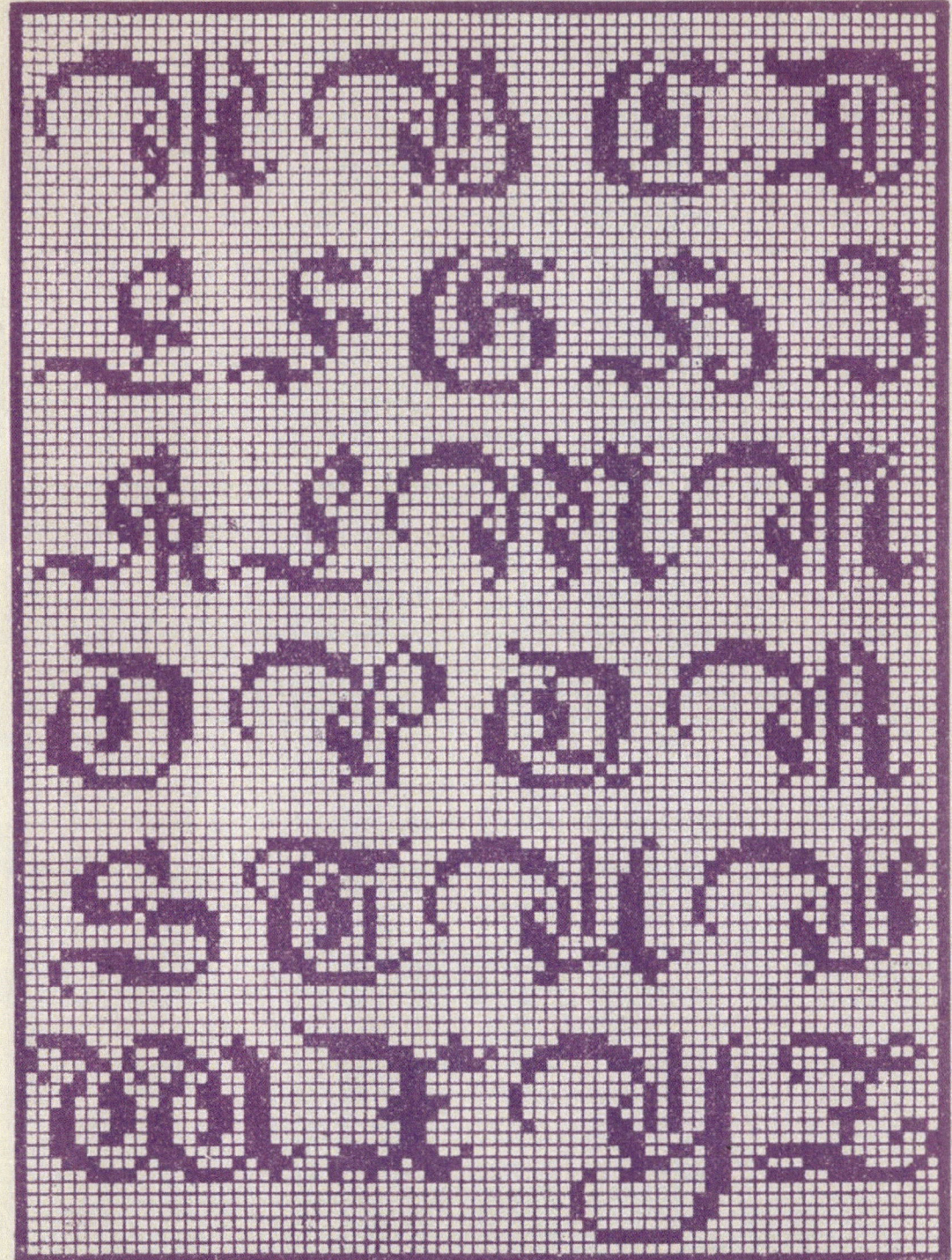

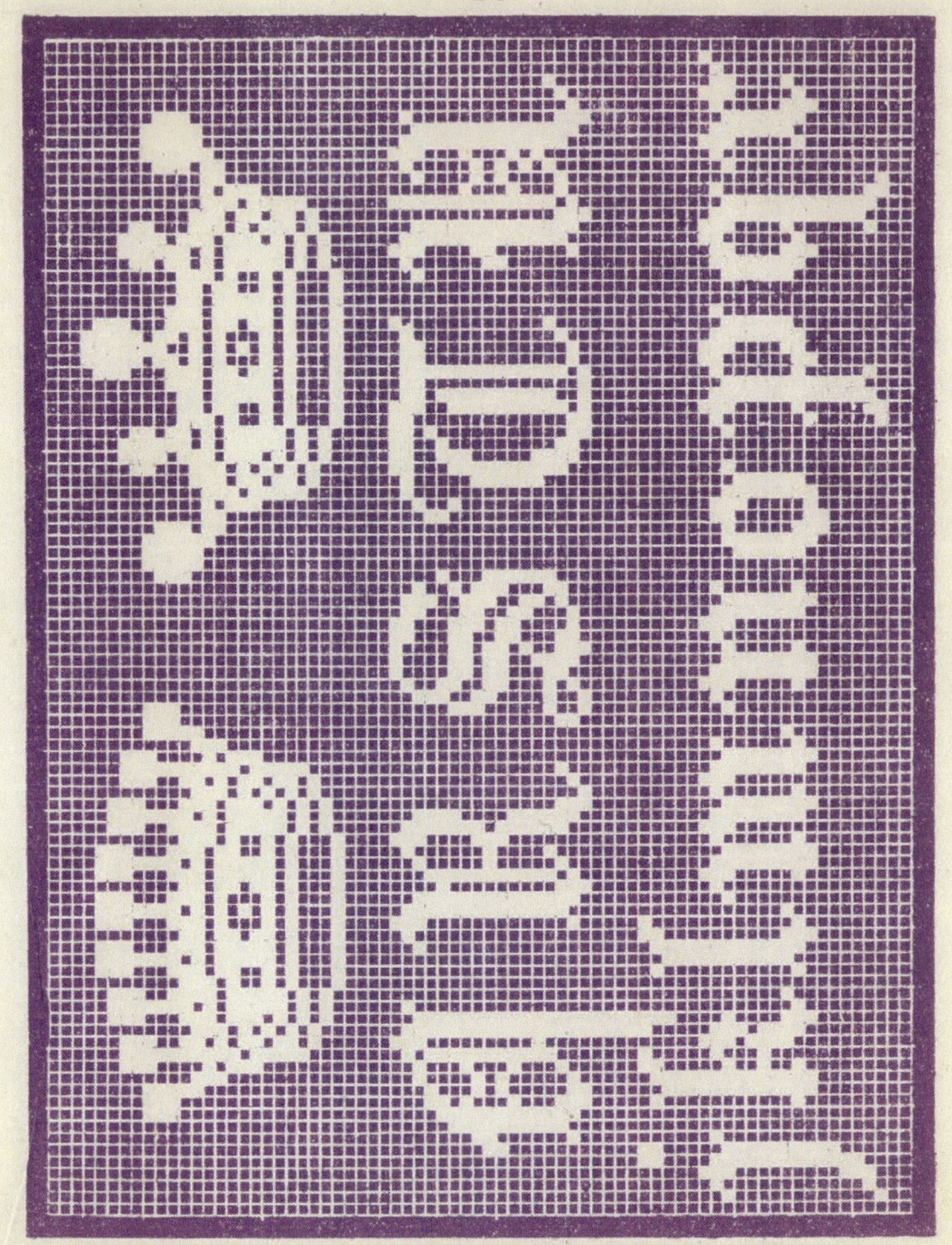

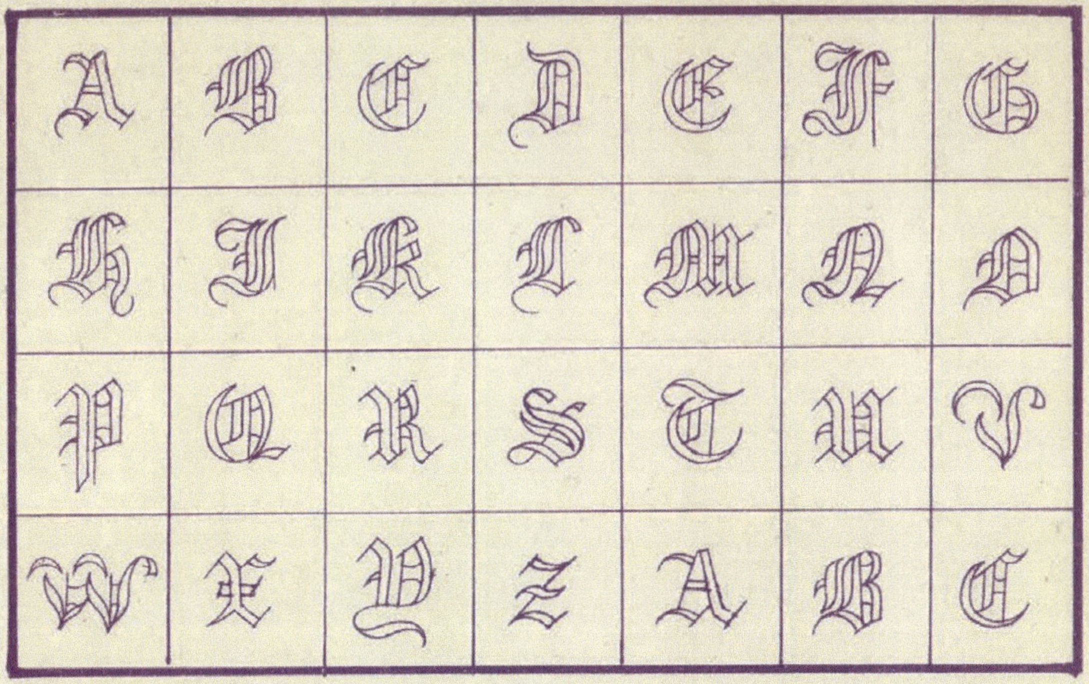

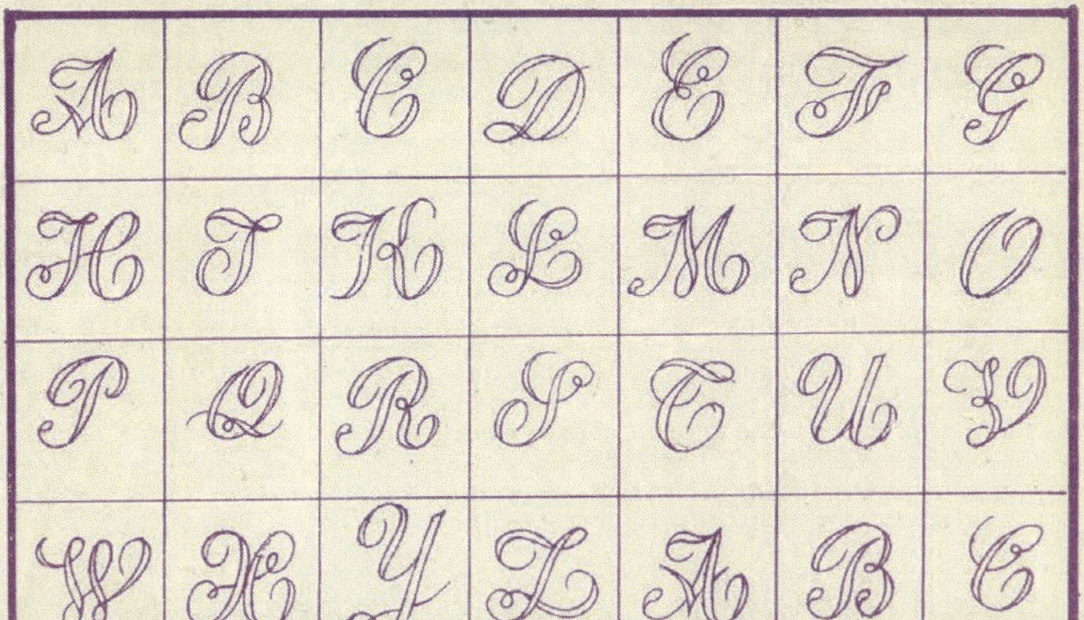

Propriété exclusive de la Manufacture Parisienne des COTONS L. V.

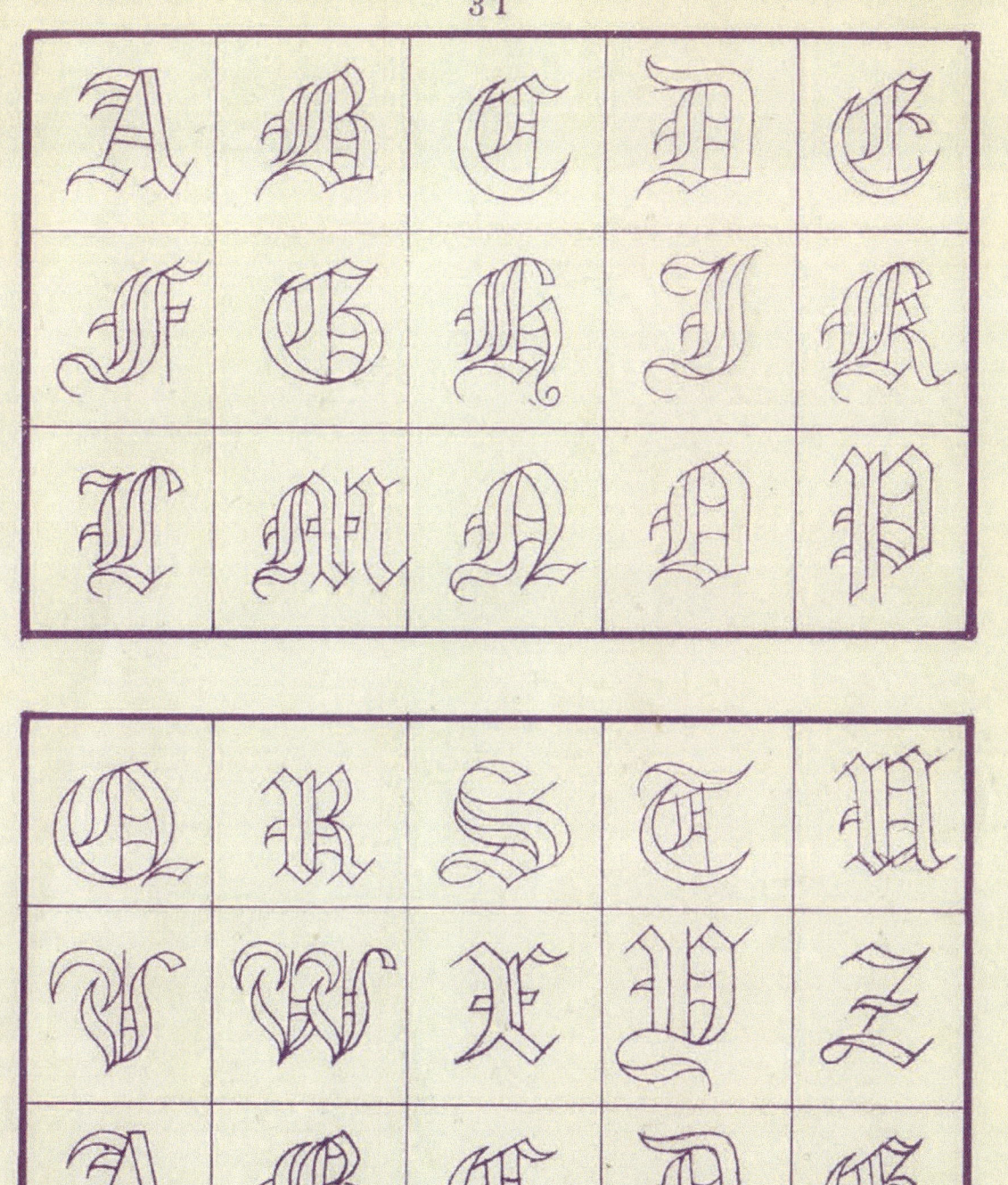

ALPHABETS from 19th CENTURY PARIS

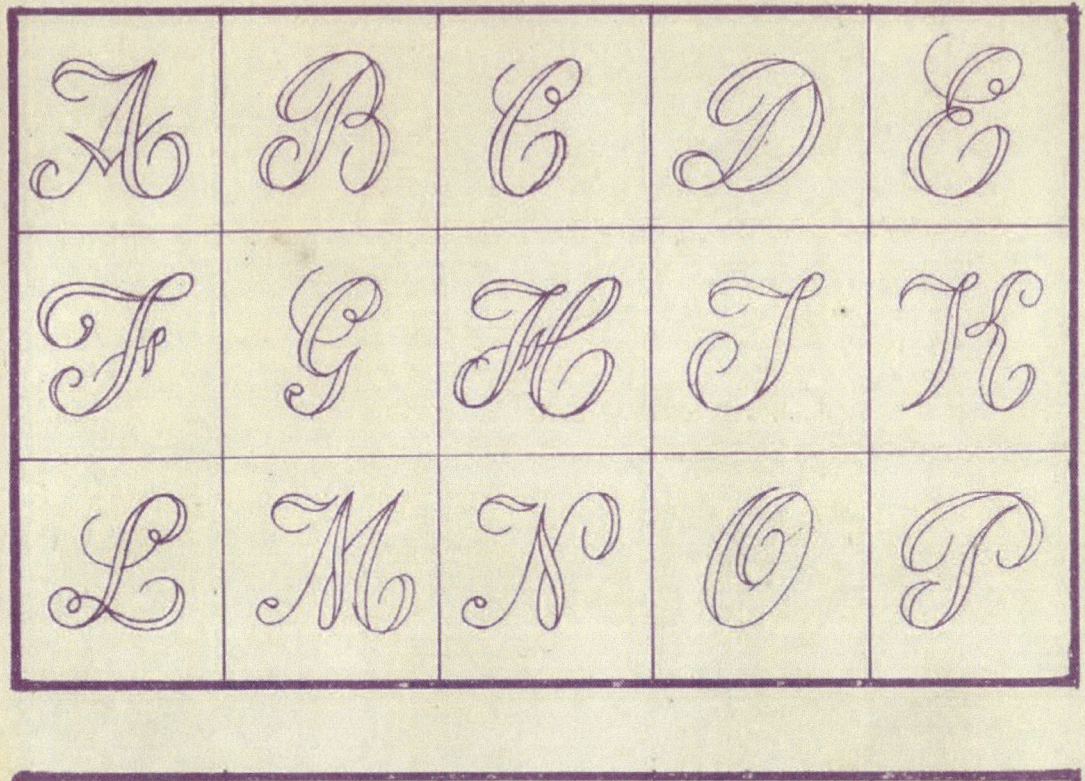

Propriété exclusive de la Manufacture Parisienne des COTONS L. V.

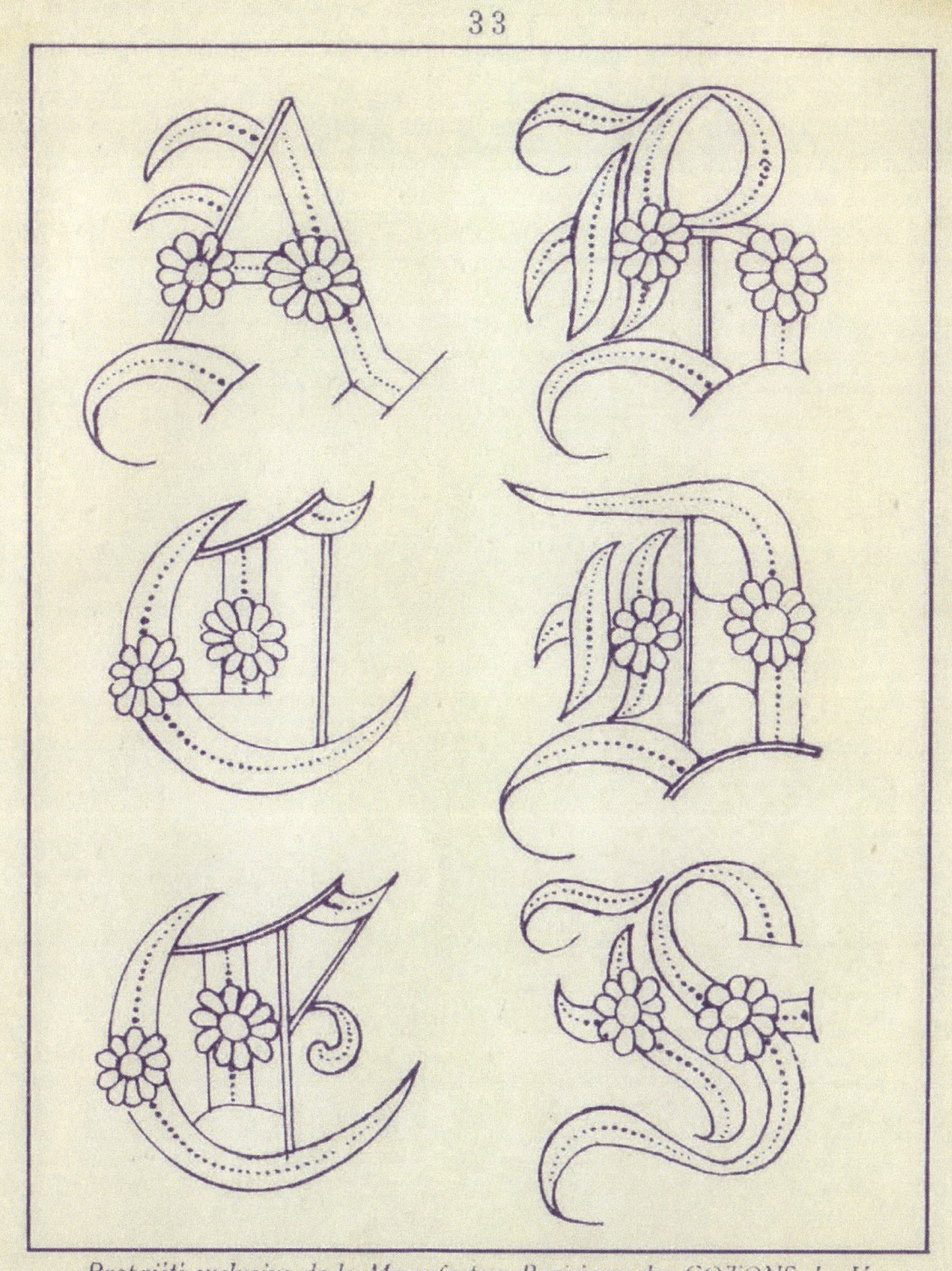

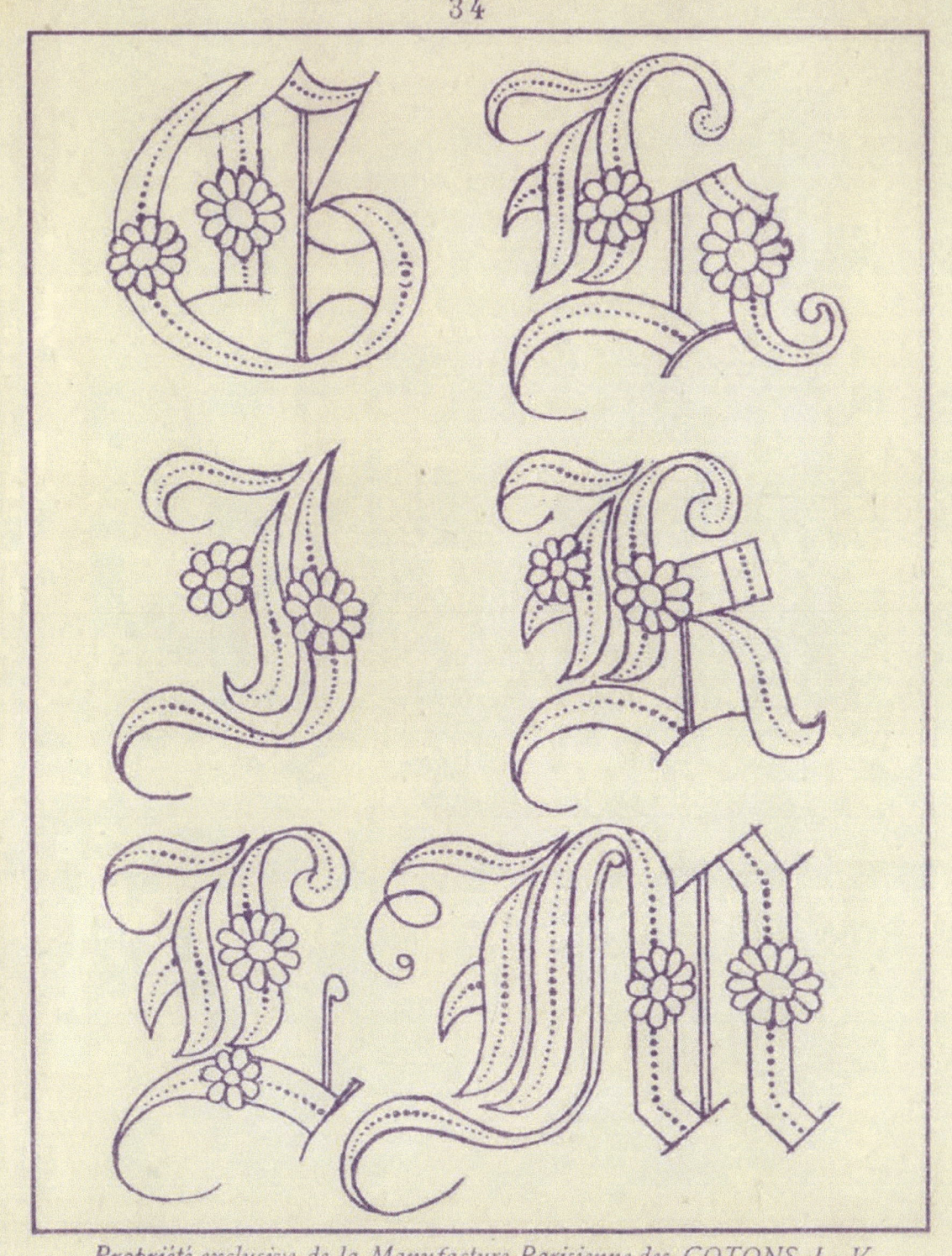

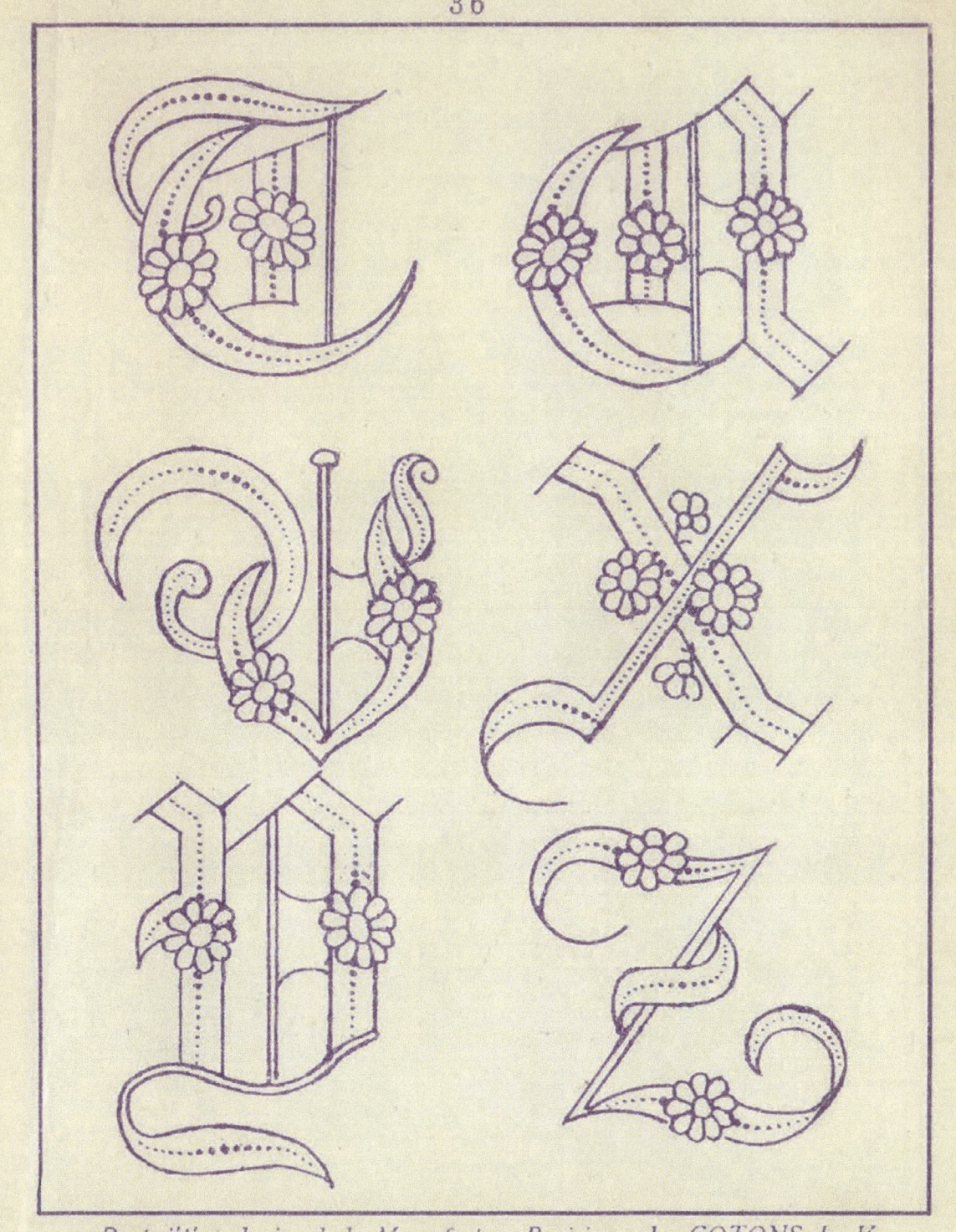

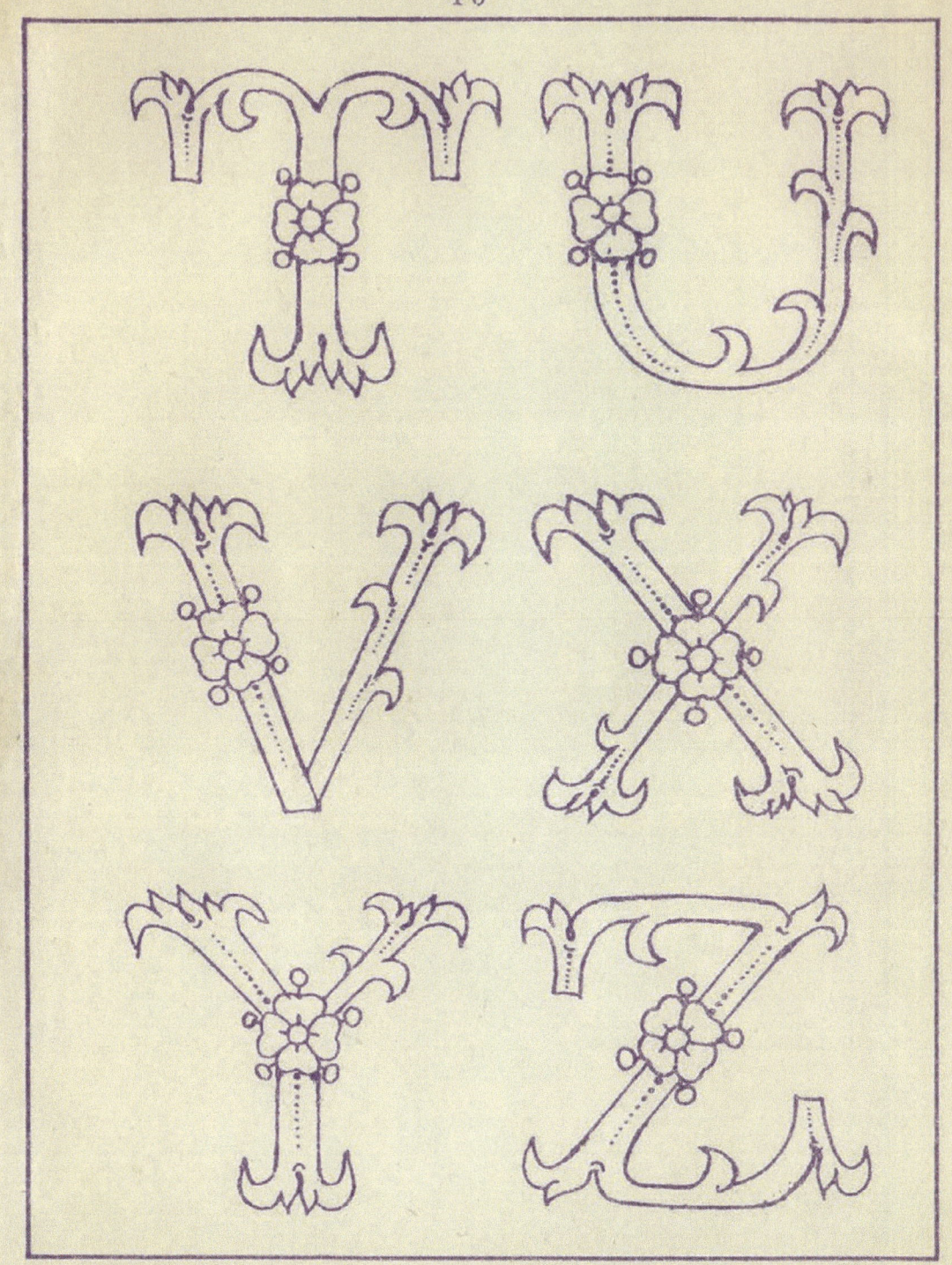

COTONS L.V. PARIS

MARQUES RECOMMANDÉES

A BRODER.... { AU PAON M.F.A.
                A LA PLUME L.V.

A MARQUER.. A LA PLUME

ARTICLES SPÉCIAUX

POUR BRODERIE DE COULEURS

ARIANE L.V. Genre SOIE D'ALGER

PHÉNIX L.V. Genre PERLÉ

Dans ces deux Marques
grand assortiment de couleurs pouvant se lessiver.

If you're an experienced stitcher, you're probably already planning how to incorporate these patterns into your next project! If you're new to working from a chart, basic techniques are described below.

"Counted thread" refers to stitching from a charted pattern instead of marking the design on your canvas or evenweave fabric– you actually "count" each individual stitch. It's much easier then that may sound! Each square on the chart represents a single stitch. These charts are shown in colors but feel free to create your own color scheme.

You'll need an evenweave ground fabric such as needlepoint canvas or linen suitable for cross stitch. Number of threads per inch determines the size of each stitch; #10 canvas (or 10 mesh or 10 count) has 10 stitches to the linear inch and 100 stitches to the square inch, so a border 10 graph squares high will be 1-inch high when stitched on that size canvas. Worked on #18 canvas (which has much smaller stitches) that same border will be only a little over 1/2-inch high.

To determine the stitched size of a pattern, divide the number of squares on the chart by the number of stitches per inch of your canvas: 10 squares high divided by 18 canvas threads per inch equals 0.55 or about 1/2-inch. Allow a minimum of 2" and preferably 3" or more of blank canvas or fabric around the stitched area to use in finishing your project.

Basic Cross stitches are shown below. Embroidery floss is the most popular thread, and you'll want to separate the plies and put back together the number needed for your fabric choice. You can work individual stitches, completing each one before beginning the next, or work a line of half crosses and then go back and complete them to create full Crosses.

CROSS STITCH
worked over 1 thread

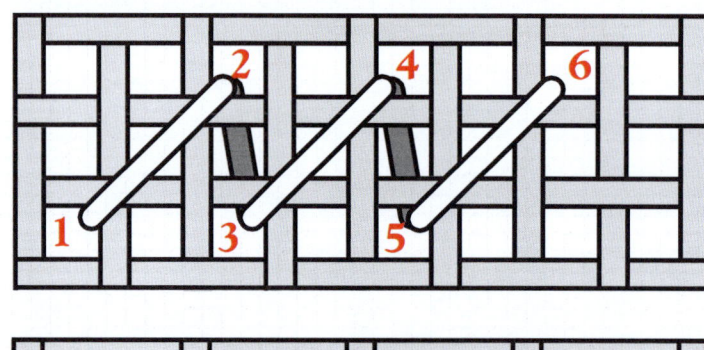

working Half Cross stitches left to right

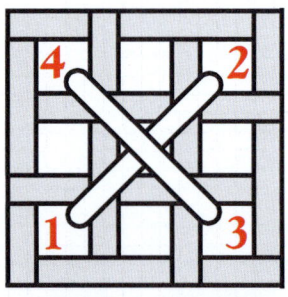

CROSS STITCH
worked over 4 threads

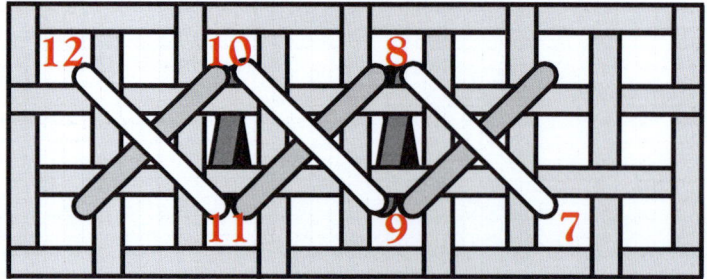

working back right to left to complete each Cross

ALPHABETS FROM 19TH CENTURY PARIS©

Needlepoint is most often worked as a *half cross* stitch, also called *Tent* or *Continental*. Worked as diagonal rows, the same stitch is called *Basketweave* and is the best choice for filling in backgrounds. Typically, you'll use thread or yarn heavy enough to fill the canvas holes and produce a smooth, solid fabric particularly suitable for pillows and rugs. The background can be filled in or the canvas left exposed for decorative projects.

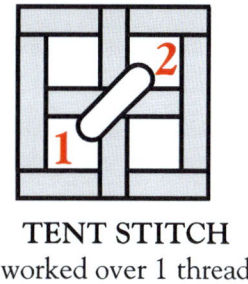

TENT STITCH
worked over 1 thread

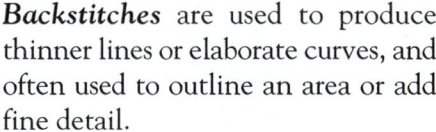

BASKETWEAVE
Tent stitches worked
in diagonal rows

working left to right

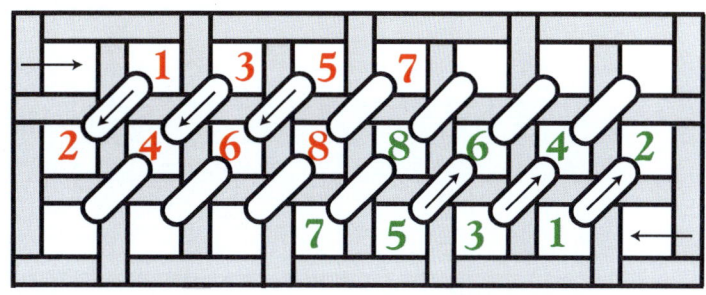

working right to left

Backstitches are used to produce thinner lines or elaborate curves, and often used to outline an area or add fine detail.

Use a thinner thread (usually only 1 or 2 plies of embroidery floss) than was used for the cross stitches, particularly when these stitches are worked on top of the Tent or Cross stitches.

BACKSTITCH
motifs and outlines

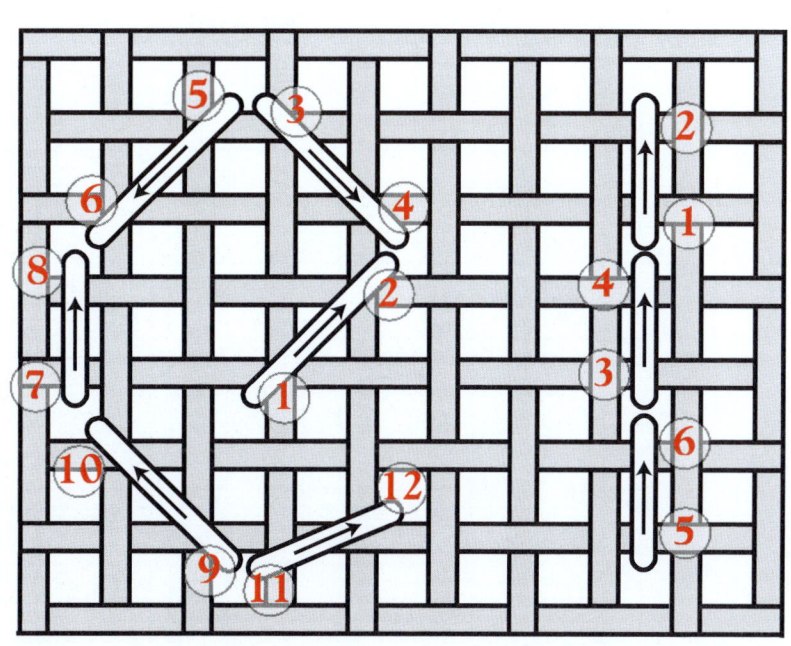

ALPHABETS FROM 19TH CENTURY PARIS©

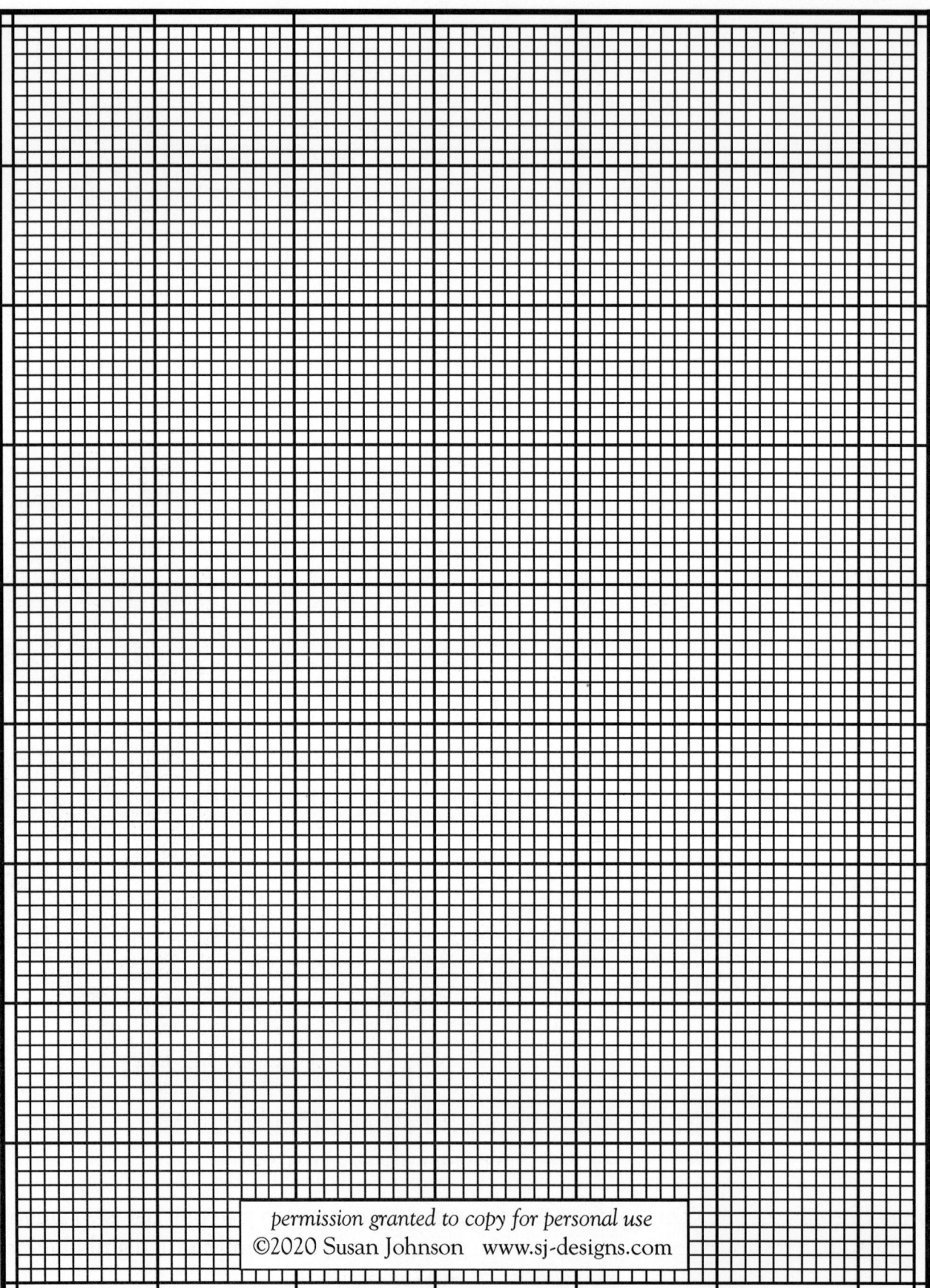

permission granted to copy for personal use
©2020 Susan Johnson www.sj-designs.com

these quality re-publications of antique needlework patterns are from the private collection of Susan Johnson

© 2020 SJ Designs All Rights Reserved.
Reproduction by any means is prohibited without written permission of the author.
Questions? Comments? Email Susan at susan@sj-designs.com.

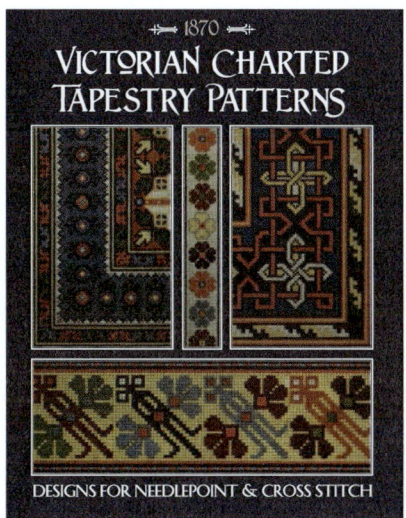
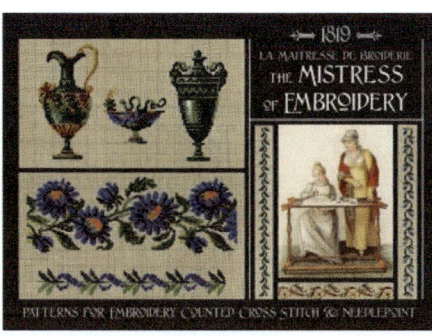

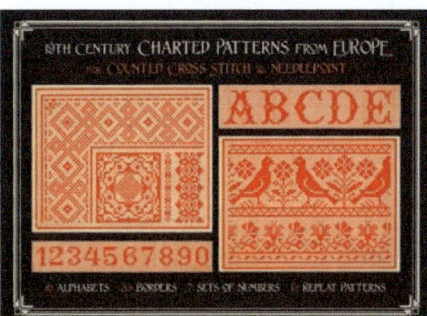

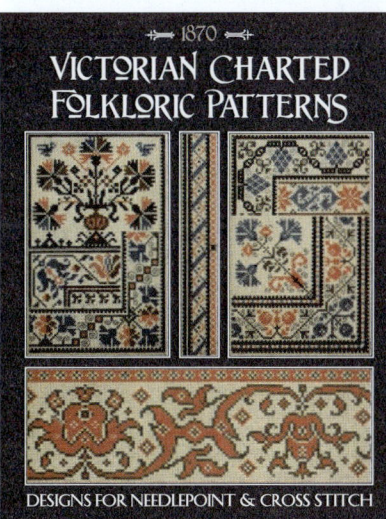

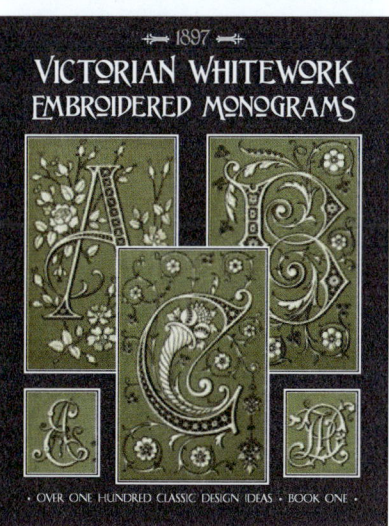

Printed in Dunstable, United Kingdom